ISIS

SETH

NUBIS

AMON

RA

Written/Artwork
LARRY CHRISTIAN
-(ANUBIS)-

ANU POETRY
COPYRIGHT 2009©

Distance Pleasures

A Poetry Book written for the soul and mind of those who are seeking love, pleasure, and life. Let these poems touch the dephts of your desires within a world of Distant Pleasures.

To order additional copies of this book, contact:
Xlibris Corporation
1-888-795-4274
www.Xlibris.com
Orders@Xlibris.com

Title: Distant Pleasures

Table of Contents

Distant Pleasures

Rhyming Poetry

"Nice An9 Slow"

Our eyes connect like the softness of a river
flow, nice and slow...
My lips caress yours tasting your essences
never wanting to let go...
Gentlely I touched your skin as you touched
mine with full control...
Our heart begain to beat as one rhythmically,
nice and slow...
The beauty of your mind is like a story that
is untold...
Mentally and physically I'll make love to
your mind, body, and soul, nice and slow.....

"When NightFall"

As I awaken to another day my heart is
filled with sorrow...
Baring the thought of being without you there
is no yesterday, today, nor tomorrow...
For every second of my life I wish I could
hold you near...
But as time pass throughout the day the
thought of missing you I shed my lonely tears...
I could only see you in my dreams and it
is to awaken that I can not bare...
If I would have died within my sleep, when
nightfall, I would not have cared because I
know within my soul that you my love would
be there.....

"Taste"

Would I be wrong if I asked you how
sweet you taste...
Kissing your lips, your neck all the way
down to the right place...
Fulfilling your every need going until you
say stop...
Becoming the hands that change every second,
minute, and hour of your clock...
Letting your rain flow as your showers
cover my body parts and face...
Will I be wrong if I told you how sweet
you taste.....

"Deep"

As your earth slowly opens, inviting me to the
richness of your soil...
I gentlely plant my seed deep within your
core as you help it through its toil...
My fingers caressed the warmth of your
grass wondering through the pleasures of your
sand...
Feeling you sliding through my fingers as I
placed you inside my hand...
As my tears of pleasure dropped on the spot
where our love has started to make this life
complete...
Though it was my flower that rosed to
the surface, it was my roots that went
inside of you Deep...

"A Peddle Of Love"

Words can not express the way that I feel,
because, our love is divine and true...
You are a gift from God, the sun within my
cloudy days a rose in the image of my Boo...
A seed tenderly planted within the softness
of the earth...
We were soul-mates destine to be together
from the beginning of our birth...
As my tears slowly fell upon the seed helping
it to grow...
A gentle kiss from my lips as life begain
to flow...
Deep within my heart and soul I knew you
was a Blessing from above...
I searched the whole world to find a rose
like yourself a beautiful Peddle Of Love.....

"Don'tStop"

Our tongues danced a forbidden dance as
I tasted the sweetness of your lips...
My hands caressed your curves as my
fingers gentlely touched your hips...
Kissing your body, savoring every single
drop...
Hearing the soft tender whispers of your
words saying, Don't stop...
Forever our soul shall stay as one, you are
the true essence of me...
The blood that flows to my heart, the most
precious words that I speak...
Entering into your body and soul making
it slowly rock...
Watching your eyes close as you gentlely
trembled, repeatly saying Don't Stop.....

"A Perfect Picture"

If I could paint a perfect picture it would
be of a golden sunset...
Visions of your beauty and the warmth of your
smile on the first day we met...
The soft tender touch of your lips, is what I
truley miss...
A gentle embrace a lovely taste with the
sweetest of kiss...
You captured my heart, mind, body, and soul...
You are the air that I breathe from my birth
until I'm old...
For every soul, God created it's perfect mate...
The day we became one, it was God's will our
fate...
I write these words to you my love with the
lonely drops of my tears...
Missing you mentally and physically, wishing you
where here...
I honor every moment with you and I'm asking
you for your trust...
Sometimes I make careless mistakes, only because
I love you so much...
My heart use to be cold and shallow, I never
understood love nor life...
But God gave me the greatest gift in the
world and that was you as my wife...
If I could paint a perfect picture it would
be of a golden sun-set...
Because you brought light to my life and
a love I will never forget.....

'Essence Of Love"

Beauty is only skin deep within the physical form...
Mentally it is to the soul and beyond...
Passion is what we feel from a tender touch, a
gentle kiss...
To stare into your eyes as my lips embrace your
lips...
A moment of pleasure a second of pain...
Our bodies shower over one another, like the
purest of rain...
For a painting can show a picture of a million
words and physically we still don't understand...
That every touch the painter used, was emotionally
done with his or her hands...
To look into your eyes means to see the world as
you do...
To taste of your lips is to only speak to you my
love, of nothing but the truth...
A moment of pleasure is to understand emotionally
that life is real...
For every second of pain, mentally and physically
I see you endure I want to know how you feel...
Our bodies shower each other spiritually in
the purest of form...
Our souls embraced emotionally like after the
pain of birth when the child is born...
Love is not always physically seeked it is seeked
mentally as well...
The Essence Of Love is spiritually given
just look into my eyes and you could tell.....

"PlanetLove"

Let me enter into your galaxies as I
taste of your milky way...
Visiting each planet embracing the essence
of your time and space...
Watching the stars dance within the twinkles
of your eyes...
Comets slowly fall, like the lonely tear drops
as life pass us by...
So many worlds unknown and yet you flow
with such perfect form...
My spaceship enter into the O of your Zone
then slowly another star is born...
The warmth of your sun that set real low is
full of life and heat...
Before I enter into your earth I caressed your
moons teasing your venus beneath...
As I flowed through your solar system nice
and slow gentlely as a dove...
I come to realize that time nor space no longer
exist when we are making Planet Love.....

"Time"

What is a clock that turns without the hands
to change its time...
What is a well verse speaker who could not
speak from the mind...
What is speed without the essence of sound...
And if a tree falls is it the tree that makes
the sound or do it comes from the ground...
A childs birth is fixed by a number of years...
Nine months is the amount she shed her loving
tears...
What is a thought without the use of our mind...
What is a clock that tick, but don't tell us the time...

Poetry Letters

"May I Touch You"

   I open this letter with the thoughts of my mind to show you a world unknown. So you may see life threw my eyes and walk the places I have gone. Though my pain you could never bare nor my struggles for truth. I could only give you a understanding on what I'm going threw. May I touch you is a womb thats been deformed, a spiritual, mental and physical state of a child reborn. May I touch you are the words that was so tenderly said. The words at a lower state of mind which made me wish I was dead. May I touch you is a phrase that ehco within my mind, a dream of control and lust. That most purest of wish inside of a fantasy world that slowly turned to dust. A seed that had landed which is planted deep (within) my earth. A mind so young within a soil never turned down know what the see is worth. May I touch you was what the world had to offer because no one eve tried to help. May I touch you came from the hands of others who didn't care if I can't touch myself.....
(A letter from the point of view of a pregnant teen girl.)

"Life"

The soft flow of my pin as I think of you is what brought these words to life. Death was upon my soul, the darkest of cloud I behold but it was you who gave me that light. As our world slowly turn and seasons changed Summer, springs into Fall. Winter breeze gives us chills because beauty was nature and all. So let me count the ways to open up your heart which was <u>locked, up</u>, trapped behind your pain. A shower of tears within a life of fears words that can't be explained. I see the hurt within your eyes from betrayal and lies and emptyness hiden deep inside. So many times I thought that I understood you but, it was you who understood me. The pain that I felt the tears that I cried the reason why I felt lonely. You had opened up your heart and soul to me hoping that it would give me sight. To see everything that a woman endured because it was you who gave the world life.....

(A letter to a woman letting her know you to feel her pain)

"Sincerely Yours"

I pray that this letter reaches you in the purest of form spiritually, mentally, and physically as well as beyond. For words can not express the undieing passion that comes from ones heart. But, if you will allow me the opportunity to try, then I shall kindle the sparks. To understand myself, first I must understand you. Your ups and down your dislikes and the things you like to do. Tell me your fantasies as well as the things that brings to you fear. Allow me to hold you close whenever you need me near. I could be a friend or a lover both at once if need to be. Let me be your heart when you're in pain and your eyes when you can't see. The gentle waves of the sea a tender breeze softly flowing across the ocean. An embracing touch of love with every single motion. Though I am not there with you in flesh and blood nor my lips can't tell you how I feel. These words that I write is from my heart to show you my love is sincere for I am Sincerely Yours.....
(This letter, if need explaining, is man given self to love.)

"Truth Hurts"

    I guess time becomes an essence when a lesson must be learned. Fire is no threat until the day you get burned. I was told a fish is very plentiful within a sea, to many to understand. But if you catch them one by one pulling them out the sea they are helpless on dry land. For years I didn't want to listen to a word you said, because, you wore the skirt. I guess my pants was to damn tight, now that you're gone the truth hurts. So many times you gave me your heart expressing how you feel. If only I would have loved you back to let you know that my love was real. A man ain't suppose to cry is the lonely words I embraced, because, this is what I was told. But, when I looked into your eyes then finally realized, that when you left, you took my soul. A second of my time was all you asked to share with me and you tried to give me the world and so much more. Though Hell was my fate you stood by my side, guiding like an angel, you walked me threw Heavens door. It took you to leave for me to see how precious you are and all you're worth. A lie is what I have Lived all my life because the "Truth Hurts.".....

(A letter of regret after loosing the love of your life.)

"My Lady"

To me you are like the moon that eloquently sits in the sky. A light that shines through the darkest of night so agressive, but yet, so shy. Surrounded by stars that slowly blink trapped within your warm embrace. So many has fallen and only a few still stand allured by the beauty of your face. To watch you slowly rise and then gentlely set is just a work of art. Your smile captivated the earth right from the start. From dust til dawn night til day you are the reason that the season change. The fullness of your glow soothe the most wildest animal at bay as the wolves call out your name. To you I write these words with love within this token of time. For you my blood flows like the ink of my pin with every single line. In my dreams I see you as forever and to be with you forever I will sleep. We share a love thats beyond the soul a love that is tender and sweet. Holding you in my arms keeping you safe as if you was a little baby. Protecting you from the sins of the worlds my most precious of perls because you are my Lady.....
(A letter explaining the love for his lady to creation)

"If Only I Could Hold You"

If I may, please allow me one chance to express to you the true essence of my mind. So you may understand the true meaning of my thoughts behind ever single line. To you letters form words and words are only spoken. But if our lips are sealed and our heart don't feel then it is the soul that would be broken. For many nights my pillow gave me warmth behind the lonelyness of my tears. I awaken for several nights wishing you was here. The beauty of your smile the softness of your skin, it was your eyes that I loved the most. A window that once was closed I could see deep within your soul for you had showed me your ghost. The same fears that I seen in your eyes was the same truth which was a lie. Now I understand the reason you have always push me away. Because of the pain from yesterday tomorrow might be another today. So don't be afraid I'm not trying to mold you. I just want to be the love that you need because you are the air I breathe If only I could hold you.....

(A letter needing to be close to that special someone.)

"Dear Love"

Let this dance be forever as you sing to me a lullaby. No more tears of pain nor shall you hurt from lonelyness so don't cry. A Queen of beauty with a mind of loyalty for no one else could compare. I'll be your knight in shinning armor one who would (die) for your love just to show you how much I care. So if it takes death to bring forth life then let me die forever. And if I was to live, then with you I shall die never. The blood of my blood the flesh of my flesh our mind and soul became one. You are my heaven and I am your earth together we brought forth a sun. Gentlely I kissed your lips as you awaken from your dream. Reality of life and love is more beautiful then it may seems. Let us leave this world and go to a place where you and I will live in the sky. Above the clouds looking down at the worlds a place where it's only you and I. A Queen for a king the most purest of doves. Without you my life no longer exist for you are my soul-mate, my true dear love.....
(A letter of a soul-mate fantasy world for the hereafter.)

"Short And Sweet"

By the time you read this letter our life will be nothing but the pass. So many lies and broken promises I knew we wouldn't last. Several nights I sat home alone, even waiting on you to call. Through my ups and down the sorrow and pains when my back was against the wall. You said you wanted to be the father of my child and a perfect husband to me. I was blind by the gentleness of your smile the charming of your ways my thoughts was trapped within my own lust. You told me nothing but lies now that I have realized that there where never any trust. Now that my eyes has opened and I can finally see, that it wasn't you who made me complete. So no longer shall I entertain your lies of promises and deceit I would told you to kiss where the sun don't shine but instead I'll make it short and sweet.....

(A letter from a woman tired of broken promises and lies)

"Intensive Heat"

Through out our life we had our ups and downs. And sometimes we even stood on shacky grounds. From arguing to pushing we've been through so much. Even when we seperated I could still feel your touch. You scream out to me words of hate when I call you at home. I screamed out the same and then slammed the phone. But what you didn't know was that my eyes was full of tears. I could tell you felt the same as your words echoed within my ears. So many nights I toste and turn in my sleep. Trying to find out how this came about to be. Awaken to see the sun rise is so different without you here. I caressed the side of the bed you use to sleep on and held your pillow near. The day you came back and knock on my door I let you in as I fell to my knees. With tears in your eyes I wrapped my arms around your waste and softly whispered don't leave. You gently smile as you bent and kissed my lips, I stood up and carried you in my arms. The warmth of our bodies the sweetest of taste I would turn over the world if anyone brought you harm. As I gently laid you onto the bed we made love between the sheets. We was trapped inside a world of pleasure, our most deepest and Intensive Heat.....

(A letter to a female showing the best of a breakup to makeup).

'When We Cried"

      The rain followed just like my tears onto an ocean of pain. Lonely thoughts of a rivers flow, gentlely starts to change. The soul of a man is the heart of his fears. While the spirit of a woman lies within the tender grace of her tears. Heaven sing songs as the earth slowly shaked. Mountains crumbled to the ground because love is our fate. The sun no longer shine as the moon went away. Planets stopped in mid air now that there is no night nor day. Flowers leaned in sorrow as the trees fell in disbelief. Passion turned into hate when the bird singed songs of grief. The worlds no longer turn, Hells fire don't burn as everything in existence died. This life we live because it is our soul we give this is what happens when we cried.....
(A letter (short) the soul-mates love for one another)

Old Folk Tales

"The Struggle"

The land of my flesh is where my flesh made me
who I once wass...
A mental bondage of fear, as that fear turned
into blood...
Once was a king who feured God, knew creation,
and man...
Demoralized by the blueness of the sky and
buried in their white sand...
A voice of many words but, none was ever spoken...
Denied the right to think a thought, unless you
was one of the chosen...
A ship that saled for many miles far as the eyes
could see...
Bodies trailed behind it's waves with faces that
looked like me...
Brought into an unknown land, a forbidden
home for many years we fought and died...
Hated for our color but, loved for our strength
we learned how to survive...
The hands that (stole us), the same hands
that tried to mold us had to let us be...
We fought over 400 years of physical slavery
now it's time to be mentally free.....

"White Knight"

When I was young I use to whatch
dem white folks standen aroun the
tre...
Screamen and yellen at someone who
looked like me...
The sound of whip cracken against
his flesh had the croud screamen white Pride...
Even doe I couldn't see thah face
I knew it was hate in thay eyes...
But the man didn't say a word nor did he
beg or plea...
The pale face man with the whipe said
since you want to help them so much then
wit them you'll be...
A thick rope was thrown over a big
limb on the tre...
As them white folks sing their hanging
song of liberty...
They placed the rope around the
mans neck and he still didn't say a word...
The rope was pulled and tied to a broken
limb within their eyes justice was served...
When everyone had left I made my way
to the tre to see the face of the man whom
they hanged...
As I saw his face I was shocked and amaze
how we were so different but yet looking threw
his eyes we were the same...
This same man helped my father and
mother, teaching our people how to read and
write...
A pale man died by the hands of his own people
all because he felt what he did was right...
His heart, mind, body, and soul is ours because
to them he was nothing not even worthy of life...
But to us he was like the other blacks that
died he was the purest of White Knights.....

"How Could We"

How could I live each day when little childrens
are dieing...
How could I be happy when our Black Queens
are crying...
How could we find love and trust in our own home...
How could I say you're a father when your always
gone...
How could I tell my mother to hold on and be strong...
How could I tell her with the family is where she
belongs...
How could we look our Queens deep into their eyes...
How could we speak the truth to them when every word
is a lie...
How could we call our beautiful black sisters by words
of disrespect...
How could we hate the color that God made so
perfect...
How could I awaken each day by God's grace and
say that I'm a King...
How could we forget as Blacks that this life is not
what it seems...
How could we allow our hopes to die within the hearts
of our mothers dreams...
How could you say that you are perfect by all means...
Your life would not be in existence if it was
not for God giving us our Black Queen.....

"If I Was To Die"

If I was to die then let it be for a cause. Let it be for caring about the sick and helping the needy lifting the weak when they fall. So if I was to die let it be for the blood of my people fighting to be equal hoping one day to be free. And if I was to die for all of the tears suffering through the years no longer shall we hang from a tree. Now if I was to die let it be for the ways of God walking in every step. If I was to die for His love and mercy then let it be for my last breath. If I was to die so that a child would live then let the Heavens sing to my soul. Because if I was to Die it would be for the future this life beholds. So if I was to die then let it be because I fought for a dream. And if I was to die then let my blood flow as freedom ring. For all of the black families who watched their loved ones hanged and killed rapped and beaten fighting back the tears as they cried. Sometimes I wish that I could have suffered for all of my peoples, but would it all be the same If I Was To Die.....

"A Pale Black Man"

      I was told that to talk with proper grammer was the ways of a white man. That I should not learn my history nor seek the truth of my people from a distant land. I was always told that black was evil a low state of mind in so many ways. But without the blackest of nights which embrace the planets there would be no day. So many times I've heard lighter skinned peoples saying I must get out of the sun before it make my skin black from the heat. But what they didn't realize that the color black is what makes a rainbow and the reflection of their skin to be. I was told by a white man that black is a color of the peoples who have been cursed. Though black is the color of every person that dies and even at the beginning of their birth. I heard so many of my peoples say that they are not from nor would they go back to the birth of their mother land. My black peoples have tried so hard not to be physically white that we have mentally became a pale black man.....

"BlackFolkMusic"

As a young child I use to hear my grandfather singing in the early morn. Sitting outside on the front porch as the sun rise watching another day being born. Words can't express his voice nor the way it sound. But if I could explain it in terms, it was like an angel softly landing on the ground. Birds sat in amazement as the Heavens held back it's thunders. The flowers rosed from a early bloom because they were in wonder. Grandpa sanged with such passion and grace words of truth and respect. Giving God all praises for life and creation and the day him and grandma first met. Deep in my soul I felt his pain and the joy that kept it at bay. To see a strong man cry with such passion in his eyes because the way we was treated in his days. So I listen as he sanged his songs and releast his soul to a world that hated him and me. As he looked at me and smiled singing the words one day you to will be free. But as a child I never understood his words nor did I knew what to do with it. It wasn't until I became a man and saw threw my grandfather's eyes that it was the soul that made Black Folk Music.

"Dirt Road"

      I remember running down the road careless and free as the heat from the sand burn my feet. Me, my sister, and brother would laugh and play all day because to us life was sweet. We use to walk on our hands as cars drove by blowing up dust in our face. It seems that time would slowly pass and in my mind there was no better place. On the far side of the road was a field where my forefathers slaved and tried hard to make a way. As they sanged songs of a better day. In those same fields there was no such thang as hand cuffs, shackles, nor words of I am better than you. Because together we struggled blood, sweat, and tears knowing what each other was going through. I looked down at the bareness of my feet dark and dry against the sand. Then visioned to myself how many of my peoples ran across this dirt road to death and freedom within another distant land. This same road is where so many blacks have died and strived to survive. The same road where we raced to our freedom fighting to stay alive. As I looked back and forth at this street to some that was called gold. A place where freedom was possible along a trail that we called a Dirt Road.....

"Prayer"

I heard so many older people saying when I was growing up, that a family who pray together stay together. Even though physically we had our ups, downs, and all in between. It was the spiritual love from our souls that made life easier then it seems. As childrens we use to watch the sun set as the moon shined with grace. As kids we wondered how things was created so perfect and tenderly put into place. Mother would walk into our room just before we go to bed. And softly tell us to pray as we bowed our head. Now I lay me down to sleep and pray to my Lord Let it be my soul He'll keep. Those words forever danced in my mind so gentle and sweet filling my soul making me complete. Mother always told us after prayer trust in God and through Him you will see another day. Just as night slowly fades our life could be taken away. As I grew from a child to a man I saw the harshness of the world when no one was there. Then I remembered what my mother told me and found peace through prayer.....

"My Father My Friend"

Tough love is what you gave to asend my soul to a higher state. Spiritual father of peace and mercy you made God my fate. To be a man of many things is what my heart desire. But you sat me down and looked into my eyes and said they only leads you to the fire. Close your eyes and feel the breeze and embrace the most purest of grace. My heart beat fast as my soul danced when a tear slowly rolled down my face. I saw visions of a life filled with joy and pain a place for you and me. Thinking back to the time we use to fish and hang out, making jokes by the tree. Physically you showed me a world I never knew to look at the things within this life by truth. Truth that comes from a Divine Source which would give me a spiritual fruite. As a father you showed me the best of both worlds. A friendship more precious than the most beautifulest of perls. You knew me better than I knew myself. Someone who was always there when I needed help. When I saw you I seen me, the things you did the way you walked. Everybody say I am you because the way I talk. You was always there for me from the beginning to the end. You taught my that black is strong and beautiful my father my friend...

"The Dream Lives On"

There was once a man who screamed from the mountain top I had a dream. A vision of a world where everyone joined hand and hand as racism had no means. A land where our mothers cried and our fathers died fighting to let liberty ring. To be equal with the race of all men was the words that they sing. To see a little black child walk down the sidewalk with a white child holding each others hand. And through the course of their lives if one shall fall the other help him to stand. To bow our heads and pray as one no matter what your religion or faith. To believe deep down within our souls that God will make this world a better place. As the man spoke with such force and strength of word which gave people soul a state of peace. The fire that burn within his eyes was of humbleness, love, and releaf. See his visions took him beyond the basic man. With God in his heart and a divine spirit to guide him his feet was placed on firm land. Though he knew his days was short for the words which was used and everyone was well spoken. Proud to be black but, live as equal with all races because he knew God had made him chosen. A king whom guided his followers to a path of honesty and might. A king whom told all of mankind to love one another and for justice together as one we will fight. But let it be a fight that will embrace the heart of every woman, child, and man. A fight which we use our mind, heart, and, soul. instead of our hands. So oh mighty soul, scream from the mountain top words of your Dream. Let everything that was created by God know the truth by all means. Deep within my soul I shall forever shed my tears because you and your beautiful wife is gone. But each day that I live I will teach my kids as I scream from the same mountain top that the king Dream Lives On.....
(In Loving Memory of Martin L. King with tears and love.)

"By Any Means"

There once was a man who looked into my soul and said be proud of who you are. He told me to love my mother and obey my father because by God they brought me this far. Love who you are and adore the color of your skin. Truth is the color of Black because everything is black within. Hold your head up high walk with strength and pride. But if you seen your brother fall, do not pass him by (or) leave him to the waste side. To be a man do not mean one who can fight with his hands but one who truely know self. A person who could use his mind as well as those hands to up lift those who need help. I was amazed how straight to the point this man word was every time he said what he said. Even when he knew about his own death he never was scared. A knight in shinning armor a worrior for every black soul. His words was spoken to the world with such passion and control. An eye for an eye never will I turn my other cheek. He show-ed me sometimes it takes one mans death for another to be complete. The man raised his hand and pointed one finger then said I respect my brothers who had a dream. With God in my heart and my brothers blood flowing threw my soul, from the mountain top I to will scream. If anyone would try to stop the will of God I will fight them to continue your dream and let it be By Any Means.....
(In loving Memory of Malcolm X. with tears and love.)

Poetry In Motion

"Chocolate Drop"

As I stare into the depts of your eyes
embracing the warmth of your soul touching you
ever so gentlely you touched me back...
A chill rushed my spine because you to have touched
my soul with your gentle breeze of lust...
The beauty of those eyes the fullness of your
lips you have trapped so many with one kiss...
A forbidden dance with the ways of your walk a
goddess that speaks a forbidden talk...
Allow my tongue to embrace your soul caressing
your boat as it slowly rocks...
Tasting your essence within my mouth the most
sweetest of Chocolate Drop.....

"Was I Wrong"

Was I wrong because I said we should think
things through..
All because I didn't give it up on the
first night now I'm sleepen with you know who...
So when you looked me in the eyes and said
you wanted us to be together...
Did you mean in the back sit of your car or in
your bed tickling my ass with a feather...
Now I remember when we was slow dancing
bumping and grinning you said I love you while singing
the song...
Well, I guess the love that you was talking about
was the little bump in your pants and if it is, that love
ain't long...
So don't get mad and use words of disrespect
because I don't have no problems with leaving you
alone...
A real man knows how to treat a lady even if she
don't take him home so now when you get to
your house little boy and take a cold shower
then think to yourself Was I Wrong.....

"Ms. Thang"

Excuse my approach but, I have to say whats
on my mind...
I found myself lost within my words within
this beautiful looken essence of divin...
So I will make my word short and sweet
very easely to explain...
A true playa been diggen you, so holla at
me Ms. Thang.....
(True words of a Pimp)

"Intro"

Hello Ms. Sunshine, may I wipe your clouds away...
To let your beautiful rays shine bringing forth another day...
Let me take away your rain as you easy my earth...
As I take away your pain and all its worth...
So I watch you from a distant within the dark all alone...
Your teardrops burning within my soul as time has slowly gone...
Other planets are afraid as they orbit around you slow...
Let my comet catch ablaze from your Intro.....

"Let Me Know"

Let me know how I can please you in every way...
Let me become the night to confur you from the heat
of the day...
Let me be the water that washes over you when you
are taking a shower...
The soft gentle drips that would last four hours...
(Drip drip drip) The sounds of your pleasure
from being soak and wet...
I tenderly kissed your lips tasting the (ones) that I haven't seen yet...
So let me guide you into a world where
your honey would flow nice and slow...
And I would do anything you want just to
please you, but only if you Let Me Know.....

"My Earth"

So many planets has crost my path, but, none have ever
marveled me like you...
Your eyes, your lips, the softness of your soil
I rose from your earth...
My tears the rain, my love the sun rays, and
my peace on a cloudy day...
As I breath upon your surfus a breeze that
would freeze your ocean...
Your earth begain to shake as your core begain
to quake you slowly opened and let me in...
The pressure of my gravity met with the
force of your energy sending vibrations through
out your lands...
As your volcano rosed and your lava flowed
shooting out in a major burst...
Let my essence confur your soul for you are my earth...

"Pause"

When I touch your soft skin ever so gentlely
I had to, pause...
As I kissed your trimbling lips so full and
sweet I had to, pause...
As we embraced and our souls became
one we had to, pause...
When I told you I love you and the
words was sincere I saw you, pause...
Tears fell from those beautiful eyes with such
love and passion my heart it, paused...
The essence of our soul was lost in a world
of pleasure as the whole world, pause...
As our body jerked from a climax beyond
words and life it self we tried to, pa..pa...pa..pause.....

"Let Me Be"

Let Me Be the waves that slowly flows
down your stream...
Gentlely falling over your edge like a water
fall splashing into Eternal Bliss...
Let Me Be the seed that is planted tenderly
inside you soil...
As my roots reach into your soul and allow
my flower to bloom from the heat of your spring...
Let Me Be the beating of your heart never
once shall I skip a beat...
Allow me to be the sweetest of taste which
makes your mouth water with pleasure and delight...
Let Me Be your honey bee who would
gentlely taste of your flower, sweet is the...
I could be your most passionate fantasy
only if you let me be.....

"Show Ya Right"

See nothing in life is free because life
ain't giving up nothing for free...
(Show Ya Right)
Time never waits for no one not even the
leaves that is on a tree...
(Show Ya Right)
A child is not born unless God allow it's
life to bee...
(Show Ya Right)
And I ain't gonna say that baby is mine just
because that baby looks like me...
(Show Ya Right)

Now if you don't want to make love I would
not be mad, baby girl I understand...
(Show Ya Right)
Just as long as I got Mary palm and her five
sisters, I'll make love to my hand.....
(say 3x) (Show Ya Right)

"WaterFall"

Let me flow the direction of your ocean
as I gentlely blow upon your waters...
Running my fingers along the warmth of your
tender waves feeling your essences flow...
Watching the sky refect in your eyes the
most beautifulest reflection of day...
And when night falls the moon dances as
the stars shine upon the elegance of your face...
As your body slowly flowed moving in one
direction I saw your soul gentely fall...
Into a stream of life and love you fell
into a beautiful pleasant Water Fall.....

(In Memory Of)

"Man In The Mirror"

June the 25, 2009 was a day when the whole world stopped. There were no rain nor sun shine not even a second, minute, or hour that moved on a clock. The earth was in pain as the world cried in disbelief. Heaven gates slowly opened for a beautiful soul it would soon keep. A life that is so precious and to us he will forever live on. You are a dimon that shines amongst the stars at night the most beautifulest song. In my mind I still could see your smile and hear the soft words of your voice as you talk. Visions of you showing me how to dance and even doing the moon walk. Never once in my life have I ever question God even in my times of fear. But on that day He took your soul I asked Him why through my lonely tears. I saw the pain within your families eyes since you've been gone and all the hurting they've been going through. I pray that God will confort them with His love and Blessings to. Let them know that he is in a better place of peace with no more worries, pain nor stress. He has gone to make a place for everyone who loved him and together we will all be Blessed. In Heaven we will see him again with a glow of the most precious of perls. A shinning light with love in his heart as the angels sing we are the world. I want to thank you and your family Michael because through you and them you all made life for me and my family dearer. For you are in me within us as we all are in you because we are a reflection of The Man In The Mirror.....

(In Loving Memories Of Michael Jackson Rest In Peace)

(Written Words To Readers, Family and Friends)

I writen these poems from my heart and soul to open up the mind and window of a world we are afraid to explore. To see our desires through the was of creation and the worlds. Three of these poems are also in loving memory of peoples who changed the lives of peoples within this world. And one day may we all see each other again in a better place. Also to my readers I thank you for taken out of your time to enter into my world through my words and see life as I do. I pray that you injoy life as you injoied my words within this poetry book. I also wrote this book in loving memories of my cusin Bo, unt Mammie Lee, and my twin Tony Christian. May God Bless you all and Rest In Peace. Once again I thank all of my friends, families, and most of God with love for my readers.

P.S.
This Book was an inspiration from
my brother Mark Shively who walked
in the same shoes as I and seen
the hardship of life as I with
much love and respect to a brother
and a friend stay strong my brother.

(Book Cover) Art Work / Written By:
Larry Christian,
(Anubis)
Poetry Book Copy: 2009/2/8 month
CopyRights @ (Distant Pleasures)

Printed in the United States
by Baker & Taylor Publisher Services